APJ Abdul Kalam — The Missile Man of India

Dr. APJ Abdul Kalam is one of the most distinguished scientist of India. He is a renowned professor, aeronautical engineer and the chancellor of the Indian Institute of Space Science and Technology (IIST).

Dr. APJ Abdul Kalam served as the 11th President of India from 2002 to 2007. He is often referred as 'People's President'. He is also popularly known as the 'Missile Man of India', because of his extraordinary contribution in the development of Ballistic Missile project and Space Rocket Technology. He also worked as a scientist in ISRO and DRDO. He was awarded with the Bharat Ratna—India's highest civilian honour in 1997.

Birth and Early Years of Dr. Kalam's Life

Dr. APJ Abdul Kalam was born in Rameshwaram (in Tamilnadu) in a middle-class Muslim family on 15th October 1931. His father was Jainulabdeen and mother was Ashiamma. Dr. Kalam's full name is Avul Pakir Jainulabdeen. His father was a devout Muslim, who had good relations with the Rameshwaram temple priests. He used to rent his owned boats out to the local fishermen. He was a good friend of the Hindu religious leaders and school teachers of Rameshwaram.

During his childhood, Dr. Kalam lived very close to the sea. He developed a great passion for nature and sea. He used to spend a lot of time watching the waves of sea. His mother influenced him to a great extent in developing his talents in music and writing poetry.

Dr. Kalam's parents led a very simple lifestyle. They imbibed good moral values in their children. Dr. Kalam became religious at a very young age. He reads 'Quran' and 'Bhagwat Geeta' daily and strictly follows vegetarian diet. Dr. Kalam devoted his entire life in doing research work.

Dr. Kalam spent most of his childhood in financial problems. His education began in a rural primary school at Rameshwaram. Later, he was shifted to Ramnathpuram Missionary School.

Dr. Kalam started working at a very early age. To bear the expenses of his education, he worked as a newspaper hawker.

His teachers, parents and others noticed his efforts and brilliance. Some of his teachers even came forward to help him.

After completing his school education in 1954, he took his graduation degree in Physics from St. Joseph College, Tiruchirapalli. In 1957, Kalam completed Bachelor of Engg. in Aerospace engineering from Madras Institute of Technology. Later he obtained advanced master and doctorate degrees in his respected field from the same institute.

Dr. Kalam's Professional Life

After completing his third year at MIT, he joined Hindustan Aeronautics Limited (HAL), Bangalore as a trainee and worked on the piston and turbine engines. In 1958, he came out of Hindustan Aeronautics Limited as a graduate.

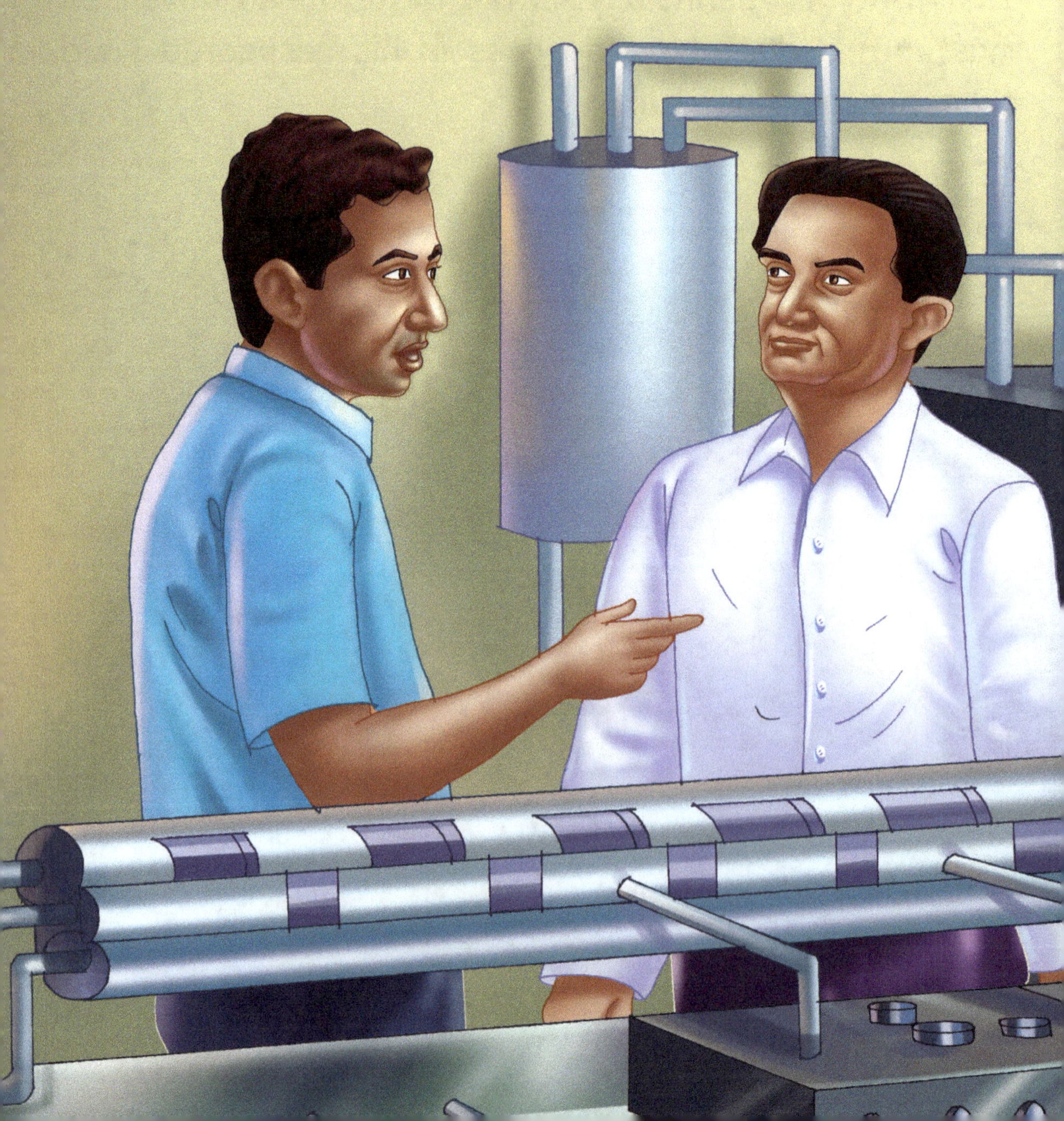

Thereafter, he got the opportunity to sewed at Indian Space Research Organisation (ISRO). After working on the several projects, he soon became a Project Director for India's first indigenous satellite launch vehicle (SLV-III) at Thumba.

The SLV-3 project was successful in placing Rohini—a scientific satellite—into orbit in July 1980 and was honoured with a Padma Bhushan in 1981. During this time, Dr. Kalam got to work with three great minds—Dr. Vikram Sarabhai, Professor Satish Dhawan and Dr. Brahm Prakash. He has also acknowledged these three people in his autobiography.

The second phase of Dr. Kalam's professional life started when he joined Defence Research Development Organisation (DRDO) in 1982. As Director of DRDO, he was entrusted with Integrated Guided Missile Development Program (IGMDP).

He played a major role in the development of many important Missiles like Nag, Akash, Trishul, Agni and Prithvi.

Three new laboratories for missile technologies were also developed during his tenure. His contributions in India's defence system are admirable.

Thereafter, Dr. Kalam worked as the Chairman of the Technology, Information, Forecasting and Assessment Council (TIFAC).

Dr. Kalam played a significant role in India's Pokharan-II nuclear test that was conducted in 1998.

In November 1999, Dr. Kalam was appointed as the Chief Scientific Advisor to the Govt. of India.
Later, in November 2001 he Joined Anna University at Chennai as a Professor of Technology and Societal Transformation.

Dr. Kalam—A Great Leader

When Dr. Kalam was working at the Rocket launching station in Thumba, there were around 70 scientists working under his leadership. To get success in their work and plan the scientists used to work for 12 to 18 hours daily. They could hardly spare any time for their families.

One day, a scientist came to Dr. Kalam and said, "Sir, I've promised my kids to take them to the exhibition going on in the town. So, I want to leave at 5.30 pm today, if you permit."

Dr. Kalam accepted his request and permitted him to leave at 5.30 pm. The scientist got engaged in his work. But when he finished the work it was almost 8.00 pm. He felt very bad that he had broken the promise given to his kids. Dr. Kalam was not in the office at that time.

In a Sad and tired mood, when he reached home he saw that his children were not at home. He asked to his wife about them. She replied, "Your Boss came here around 5.00 pm and took our kids for the exhibition."

The scientist was overwhelmed by the sweet gesture of his boss. Actually, Dr. Kalam saw that the scientist was engrossed in a very important work. And, he didn't want to disappoint the kids. So, he decided to take his children on his behalf for the exhibition.

Such an understanding and caring boss was Dr. Kalam.

Dr. Kalam as the President of India

The entire nation was surprised when the ruling NDA Government nominated Dr. Kalam—the famous scientist—as their candidate for the President elections. He won the election by huge margin and became the 11th President of India on 25th July 2002.

In his speech during the oath taking ceremony, Dr. Kalam said that we should be proud of our country, "In the last 50 years, India has made many achievements in the fields of food production, health sector, higher education, media & mass communication, information technology, science and defence. In spite of these advancements, a large population is still struggling with the problems like poverty, unemployment, diseases and lack of education."

Dr. Kalam expressed his vision to eradicate all the problems from the country and making it the strongest nation one day.

During his tenure, Dr. Kalam worked especially in the fields of science and education. He was remained as an approachable and humble President. He is very fond of the children and is always concerned for their development and welfare. He aimed to make India a scientifically strong nation and always tries to ignite the spark in the minds of Indian citizens.

Dr. Kalam has a multifaceted personality. Apart from being a great scientist, he is also interested in the field of arts and culture. He has written many books including his autobiography, 'Wings of Fire'. Some of his famous books are: 'Scientist to President', 'Ignited Minds: Unleashing the Power Within India', 'India 2020' etc.

He has also written Tamil poetry. Dr. Kalam is good at playing the Indian musical instrument 'Veena'.

Dr. Kalam has three visions. His first vision is freedom. He said that our country was ruled by many and remained dependent for a long period but we the Indians respect other's freedom, thus India has great values and culture.

Dr. Kalam's second vision is development. He said that though we have achieved a lot in the last few years, but we need to have more development, especially in the fields of education, science and technology.

His third vision is that India must be strong and emerge as a super power. It should stand up to the world and show its strength.

Dr. Kalam wants to make India an advanced and technologically developed nation. In his book, 'India 2020', he has mentioned an action plan to make India a knowledge superpower and a developed nation by the year 2020.

Dr. Kalam has been awarded with Bharat Ratna (1997), Padma Vibhushan (1990), Padma Bhushan (1981) and also received many more prestigious honours and awards.

He is presently the Chancellor of the Indian Institute of Space and Technology and also works as a professor at Anna University (Chennai) and as a visiting faculty in many academic and research institutes through out the country.

In May 2011, Dr. Kalam started a new mission for the Indian youth. 'What Can I Give Movement', is a unique mission to inculcate the Universal spirit of giving in the youth.

For years, Dr. Kalam has been inspiring many lives, especially the youth and children. He is the ocean of knowledge. We should draw inspiration from his life and must work to make India- a strongest nation.

On July 27, 2015, Dr. Kalam died after collapsing, while delivering a lecture at IIM, Shillong, Meghalaya. He was 83. The whole Nation mourned on his death, and paid homage, includes the President, the PM and other dignitaries, to him.

Birth and Early Years of Netaji's Life

Netaji Subhash Chandra Bose is considered as one of the most dynamic and revolutionary leader of Indian freedom struggle. He made and led the Azad Hind Fauj against the British rule and other western countries during the World War II. He was well known for his extraordinary courage and bold personality.

Netaji was born in a Bengali family on 23rd January 1897 in Cuttack, Orissa. His parents were Janakinath Bose and Prabhavati Devi. He was ninth of the fourteen children of his parents. His father was a successful advocate. Netaji was highly influenced by Swami Vivekanand and his teachings. During his college years, he attended many discourses of Swami Vivekanand.

Netaji was a brilliant student. He completed his school education in Cuttack. He was the topper of the Matriculation examination in the entire Calcutta province. In his student life, Netaji was known for his patriotic zeal. In his school, there used to be a lot of racial discrimination. The local students were target of the English students. The English boys always used to insult and torture the Indians.

One day, an English boy screamed at an Indian boy who touched his book. He said, "You black monkey! How dare you touch my book with your dirty hands."
The Indian boy was frightened. He could not say anything. He quietly listened to all the insulting remarks of the English boy. Netaji who was witnessing the incident, became very angry.

After the class, Netaji asked the Indian boy, "Why didn't you reply back to that English boy? He insulted you so badly!"
The Indian boy told Netaji that the English boy's father was a senior government officer. There could be negative consequences, if he would have fought with him.
Netaji was furious at the English boy. He confronted with him. The English boy made racial remarks on Netaji also. Netaji then caught him by his collar and thrashed him. The English boy fell on the ground.

This incident clearly proved that Netaji didn't fear from anyone. Since childhood, he was concerned about the dignity of his country and the countrymen.

Another such incident happened when Netaji was in college.

One day, a British professor made a racist remark on Indian students. Netaji became very angry and he beat the professor for the remark. After this incident, Netaji was expelled from the college.

Thereafter in 1918, he took a degree in philosophy from the University of Calcutta.

Netaji's parents wanted him to appear in the Civil Service Examination. To fulfil their wish, he went to England in the year 1919. He became successful and stood fourth in the merit of the Civil Service Examination.

Netaji had been a rebel since his childhood. He was against the British Rule in India. He didn't want to work under Britishers. When he came to know about Jalianwala Bagh Massacre in Punjab, he left his Civil Service apprenticeship and came back to India.

Netaji with Congress

On returning back to India, Netaji joined the Indian National Congress in Calcutta. He worked under the leadership of Deshbandhu Chittranjan Das. Netaji worked very hard to enlighten the youth and labour of Calcutta. Soon, he became a popular youth leader.

In November 1921, the Prince of Wales came to India to visit the country. The Indian National Congress decided to raise a protest against his visit. In Calcutta, Netaji organised a mass boycott to welcome the Prince.

In December 1921, Netaji and Chittranjan Das both were arrested and then imprisoned for six months. After their release, they continued working for their mission. The British Government was shocked to see Netaji's aggressive approach.

In 1924, Netaji stood for the municipal elections of Calcutta Corporation. He was elected as the Chief Executive and Chittranjan Das became the Mayor of Calcutta.

Soon, Netaji declared khadi in place of British mill-made cloth as the official dress. It was his first expression of the protest. The use of khadi was banned and Netaji was imprisoned in the Burma's Mandalay prison. This place was famous for its worst hygienic conditions. Netaji contracted Tuberculosis in the prison.

While Netaji was still in prison, his mentor and political guru Chittranjan Das passed away on 16th June 1925. Netaji was completely broken on hearing the news.

The following year, the State Council Election were held in Bengal. Netaji fought the election from the prison. He was declared elected from the Calcutta constituency. After a massive public protest and Netaji's hunger strike, he was finally released from the prison.

Netaji returned to Calcutta after his release in 1927. People, especially the youngsters, were very happy on his return.

In December 1927, Congress held its annual session in Madras. Netaji and Jawahar Lal Nehru were elected as General Secretaries of the Party.

Netaji was in favour of using violence and force to attain complete freedom. He opposed the Dominion status for India that was declared by the Congress. He said that, "We need complete independence and nothing else!"

He made a separate group named 'The Forward Bloc' within the party. This group organised nationwide rallies and protests. Because of this, he had disagreements with party officials. Finally, he left the Indian National Congress.

For his revolutionary thoughts, Netaji was imprisoned during the Civil Disobedience Movement in 1930. Netaji was exiled from India to Europe. But he used this opportunity and tried to establish political and cultural ties between India and Europe.

During his Vienna journey, he wrote a book, 'The Indian Struggle'. The book was published in November 1934. During the writing of this book Netaji met Miss Emily Shenkil. She assisted him in his writing. In 1937, Netaji got married to her. He could stay with his wife only for a month. Thereafter, he returned to India.

Netaji was arrested several times by the British Government. Later, he was kept in house arrest in Calcutta.

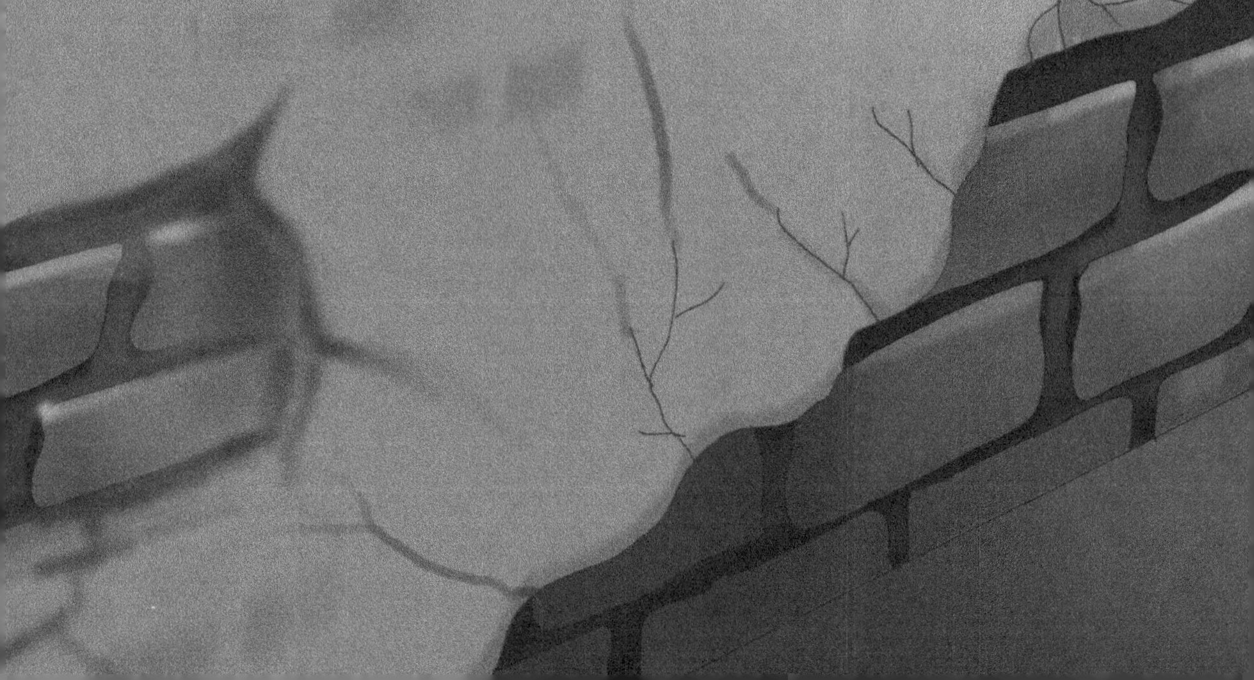

Netaji Forms the Indian National Army

At the time of the World War II, British were under the pressure of Adolf Hitler of Germany . Netaji took advantage of the situation. Disguised as a Pathan (Pashtun), he fled from Calcutta to Peshawar in 1941. From there, he went to Kabul and then to Moscow.

Netaji's next destination was Germany. He reached there and met Hitler. He told Hitler about his cause. Hitler was quite impressed by Netaji and promised to help.

In 1941, Netaji went to Japan. He got the support of Germany and Japan for his fight against the British rule in India. In 1943, he moved to Singapore and formed the Indian National Army (INA). The army was also called the Azad Hind Fauj. Netaji became the Commander-in-Chief of the Azad Hind Fauj.

The army comprised mainly of the Indian prisoners of war (POW).

There were around 40,000 soldiers. The army was made up of four brigades—The Nehru Brigade, The Gandhi Brigade, The Subhash Brigade and The Azad Brigade. There was also a women's unit named Rani Jhansi Regiment. It consisted of 100 women soldiers.

Netaji prepared the army for the battle. In 1944, INA crossed the Burma border and reached India. It waged a battle against the British Rule from the Northwest part of India. The army enthusiastically moved forward with the battle cry, 'Chalo Dilli!'

During the World War II, Germany and Japan were defeated. Because of this, the Azad Hind Fauj battle was not a success, but Netaji conveyed the message to the British. The British Government realised that Indians can go to any extent for the freedom of their country.

In one of his inspiring speeches, he said, "Tum mujhe khoon do, main tumhein azadi doonga!" (Give me your blood, and I'll give you freedom!). This quote of Netaji became very popular and inspired the Indians to a great extent.

Netaji also visited England. He met many significant political leaders. He also discussed about the future of the Indian freedom movement with them.

Netaji's Disappearance

On 18th August 1945, Netaji was travelling in a private plane to Tokyo, Japan. Over Taipei, Taiwan, the plane caught fire and crashed. Netaji was declared dead in the plane crash. But later, it was found that Netaji's body was not there among the victims.

A lot of questions and doubts were raised about Netaji's death. A special committee was also formed to investigate the truth. But no evidence of his death was found. Some people believed that Netaji was alive even after the incident. However, no strong evidence was there. Hence, Netaji's death has been a mystery for India.

Netaji Subhash Chandra Bose left a strong impression on the minds of Indians. Unfortunately, he could not witness the moment of Indian independence, for which he struggled very hard.

Netaji Subhash Chandra Bose played a very significant role in the freedom movement of India. His inspirational words, quotes and speeches are still remembered and ignite patriotic emotions in the Indians.

We can learn a lot from Netaji's life. His qualities like- patriotic zeal, courage and boldness are unmatchable.